D0243395

STONE AGE NEWS

AUTHOR: FIONA MACDONALD  CONSULTANT: ALISON ROBERTS

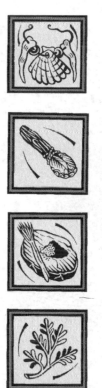

DEAR READER,

TO BRING YOU THIS SPECIAL EDITION OF *THE STONE AGE NEWS*, WE HAVE PLUNDERED OUR ARCHIVES FOR THE VERY FINEST STORIES IN THE HISTORY OF OUR NEWSPAPER.

AND WHAT ASTOUNDING STORIES THEY ARE! THEY COVER ALL THE GREATEST TRIUMPHS OF OUR PAST, RANGING FROM OUR FIRST STEPS OUT OF AFRICA, TO OUR SURVIVAL THROUGH THE ICE AGES. AND THAT'S NOT ALL. IF YOU'RE AFTER TIPS ON TOOL-MAKING, REPORTS OF DRAMATIC ANIMAL HUNTS, OR GUIDES TO STONE AGE FOOD AND FASHION, THIS AMAZING COLLECTION WILL HAVE THE ARTICLE FOR YOU!

WE'VE HAD GREAT FUN DIGGING UP ALL THESE TERRIFIC STORIES. NOW IT'S YOUR TURN TO ENJOY THEM!

Fiona Macdona

THE EDITOR-IN-CHIEF

ALLEYN'S SCHOOL

00007113

A NOTE FROM OUR PUBLISHER

Of course, as we all know, newspapers didn't exist as long as 10,000 years ago. But if they had, we're sure that *The Stone Age News* would have been the one everybody was reading! We hope you enjoy reading it, too.

Walker Books

WALKER BOOKS
AND SUBSIDIARIES
LONDON · BOSTON · SYDNEY

CONTENTS

ABOUT THE DATES

ALL OF THE events in this book happened long before there were any written records, or historians to keep them.

Experts have had to piece their knowledge together from the tools and other clues that our very first ancestors left behind them.

New evidence about the Stone Age is being uncovered all the time, and this can alter our understanding of when things happened. So all the dates that are given in this book are based on what the experts have discovered *so far*.

Historians use various ways of counting back to events that happened a long time ago.

In this book, dates are counted in years BC — meaning years "Before Christ". So 8,000 BC, for example, means 8,000 years before the birth of Christ, or in other words, almost 10,000 years before today.

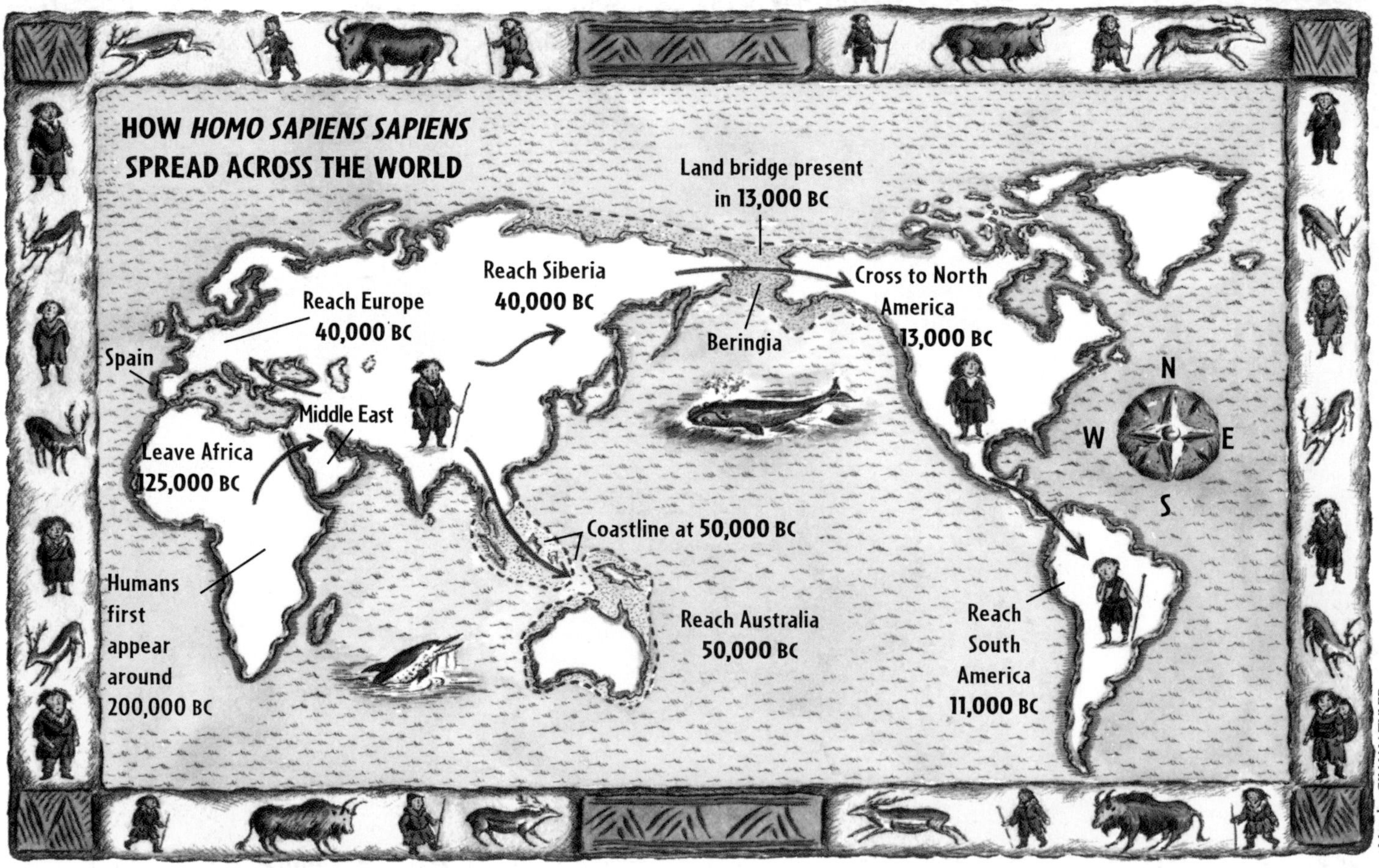

HOW *HOMO SAPIENS SAPIENS* SPREAD ACROSS THE WORLD

Land bridge present in **13,000 BC**

Reach Siberia **40,000 BC**

Cross to North America **13,000 BC**

Beringia

Reach Europe **40,000 BC**

Spain

Middle East

Leave Africa **125,000 BC**

Humans first appear around **200,000 BC**

Coastline at **50,000 BC**

Reach Australia **50,000 BC**

Reach South America **11,000 BC**

N W E S

Map by GILLIAN TYLER

OUT OF AFRICA

Illustrated by CHRIS MOLAN

NEW HORIZONS: A Stone Age family group stands on the threshold of a new world. Behind them lies Africa — ahead, an unknown land.

ALTHOUGH TODAY, in 8,000 BC, our people are scattered right across the globe, this was not always the case. In 125,000 BC, a reporter from *The Stone Age News* recorded our first momentous journey — out of Africa.

WHEN I WAS told that some of our people were planning to travel to new lands, I decided to follow them to witness the great event for myself.

Like the travellers, I set out early in the morning, to walk during the coolest part of the day.

I caught up with one family group just after they had reached the far side of the straits that separate Africa from the Middle East.

After we'd exchanged greetings, I congratulated the group on their bold step into the unknown.

"Who us? We're not brave," was their startled reaction. It seemed quite natural to them to be travelling, and the fact that they were heading into new lands did not strike them as being courageous or unusual.

A PEOPLE ON THE MOVE

We Stone Age people are always travelling, of course, tracking down animals and gathering plants for food. But this has never led us to leave Africa — until now.

This great country has been our homeland for as long as anyone can remember — ever since we first appeared on Earth, in fact!

Sadly, the records of *The Stone Age News* don't go back to the earliest days of our people. But most experts think that we modern humans — or *Homo sapiens sapiens*, as they like to call us — began life in East Africa back in 200,000 BC.

In the beginning there would have been very few of us. But our numbers have increased steadily, and today our population is around 100,000 strong.

What's more, we're an adventurous lot. And our endless search for new hunting grounds has already led us to wander far and wide throughout Africa.

And now, as the first few groups head off into unexplored lands, an exciting new chapter of the story is beginning.

The Stone Age News **will be following their progress and bringing you exclusive, up-to-the-minute news every step of the way.**

THE NEANDERTHALS

Illustrated by CHRISTIAN HOOK

NO BONEHEADS: Neanderthals were skilful tool-makers and successful hunters.

IT'S HARD TO imagine, but we once shared our lands with an entirely different people, called the Neanderthals. While our numbers grew, theirs fell — until finally, as this report from 28,000 BC reveals, they seemed to disappear altogether.

NEWS HAS JUST reached us that the dead body of a Neanderthal man has been discovered in a cave in southern Spain.

The evidence suggests that the man had been living alone there for some time, and that he died of old age.

It has been years since *The Stone Age News* reported any sightings of these people. But our records do confirm that they were last seen in areas of Portugal and southern Spain. And now our experts think it's possible that this man was not only the last member of his family group, but also the very last of his kind.

IN MEMORY

As far as we know, the Neanderthals appeared in around 250,000 BC — long before our own people — and were once widespread in Europe and the Middle East. So it seems quite incredible that they could all just vanish from the world!

Here at *The Stone Age*

SO WHAT HAPPENED?

NEWS ABOUT THE Neanderthals' disappearance gave rise to a number of theories on what may have happened to them. In 28,000 BC, *The Stone Age News* asked the experts if any of these ideas were true.

⊙ *THEORY ONE:*
They died out because we killed them all off.
We have no evidence of any violent clashes with the Neanderthals. They were peace-loving and far more likely to run away than to fight.

⊙ *THEORY TWO:*
We drove them away from the best hunting
grounds, and this meant that they couldn't find enough food to live on. It is certainly true to say that we usually managed to drive the Neanderthals away from the best hunting and gathering lands. But we cannot know for sure whether or not this actually caused them to starve to death.

GO MISSING!

News, however, we've come to accept that this is probably the case.

So, out of respect for this vanished people, we have put together the following portrait of their way of life.

SIGNS: A spear and scrapers found at an abandoned site may be the last traces of Neanderthal existence.

THE SAME, BUT DIFFERENT

Like us modern humans, the Neanderthals were nomads who wandered from place to place, hunting animals and gathering plants to eat. In fact, it was probably while searching for new hunting grounds that our early ancestors first came across them.

Apart from being a bit shorter and a good deal stockier, they were quite like us to look at.

Their way of living appears to have been something like ours, as well. They used many of the same kinds of tools as we do, and often made their homes in caves. They lived in family groups, cared for the sick and elderly, and buried their dead.

But we never came to know them all that well. One reason for this was that they had a different language from us, which made it impossible for us to communicate.

The other was that we very rarely had any contact with them.

All the reports we have of them indicate that they preferred to avoid meeting us. So if ever we moved into an area where they were hunting or living, they beat a hasty retreat — usually towards more mountainous lands.

As time went on we saw less and less of them, and now it seems we'll never see them again.

SPOT THE DIFFERENCE

FEW OF US have ever come face to face with a Neanderthal, of course. So were they any different from us, and if so, in what ways? *The Stone Age News* dug deep into its archives to compile the following check-list:

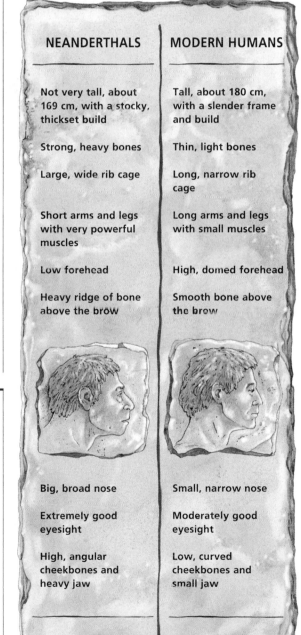

NEANDERTHALS	MODERN HUMANS
Not very tall, about 169 cm, with a stocky, thickset build	Tall, about 180 cm, with a slender frame and build
Strong, heavy bones	Thin, light bones
Large, wide rib cage	Long, narrow rib cage
Short arms and legs with very powerful muscles	Long arms and legs with small muscles
Low forehead	High, domed forehead
Heavy ridge of bone above the brow	Smooth bone above the brow
Big, broad nose	Small, narrow nose
Extremely good eyesight	Moderately good eyesight
High, angular cheekbones and heavy jaw	Low, curved cheekbones and small jaw

► THEORY THREE:
We infected them with our diseases, and the Neanderthals died out because their bodies couldn't fight off the new illnesses.
This theory is highly unlikely. If they were going to die this way, it would have happened long ago — after all, we lived beside them in the same lands for thousands of years!

► EDITOR'S NOTE:
Our experts asked us to point out that no one really knows why the Neanderthals died out. In fact, at this point in 28,000 BC, there may even be a few still living in some remote place.

ICE AGES: THE COLD FACTS

Illustrated by MAXINE HAMIL

During an ice age, temperatures around the world are much lower than normal and even the hottest countries cool down.

❄

As the Earth gets colder, vast sheets of ice, up to 3,000 metres thick, spread outwards from the ice-caps at the North and South Poles, blanketing both land and sea.

❄

Much of the Earth's water turns into ice. The oceans shrink, and new areas of coastland appear as large parts of the seabed are uncovered.

❄

Lands not covered by ice-sheets suffer from drought, as water is frozen into the ice-caps and very little rain falls to replace it.

Very few animals can survive in the regions closest to the ice-caps and most move on to warmer areas.

❄

Human groups can survive near the ice-caps by using clothing and shelters to keep themselves warm. But when the animals that they hunt for food move on, they are forced to follow them.

❄

Ice ages vary in length from several thousand years to just a few hundred. They tend to start very slowly, but end rapidly.

❄

No one is certain why ice ages happen, but experts believe they are caused by changes in the way that the Earth moves around the Sun.

TIME TO GO: As the weather worsens, people in central Russia head south.

ICE CREEPS

Illustrated by LEE MONTGOMERY

WE ALL MOAN about today's weather, but we've got it easy. There can be nothing worse than living at the peak of an ice age, as this report from 16,000 BC shows!

IN ALL MY years as *The Stone Age News'* weather reporter, I've never known cold quite like this.

The ice-sheets that stretch out from the North and South Poles are slowly but surely growing bigger. There seem to be hardly any regions where the winters aren't getting longer, and the summers cooler!

Take the north-east of Europe, for example. No one can remember a time when it wasn't a barren, icy wasteland. It's hard to believe that all sorts of plants and animals once flourished there.

And now the ice-sheets are creeping even further south, over the plains of central Russia. Recently, I travelled to

the Russian plains to find out how people were coping with the ever-worsening climate. It was only late summer, but harsh winter storms were already beginning to beat down upon the land, and there were few living creatures to be seen.

THE WINTER IS COMING

When at last I found a family group, they were packing up and preparing to move south. Looking thin and drawn, they told

PASSING PLACES

ONE OF THE most astonishing things to have happened in the last major ice age was the appearance of a land bridge linking Asia to North America — a stepping stone between two continents. Today it no longer exists, but the effect it had on our world was astounding.

DURING THE last ice age, which began in 23,000 BC, much of the Earth's water froze into ice-sheets. As a result, sea levels fell along many coasts, and huge parts of the seabed were uncovered.

One such newly dry area of land was known as Beringia. It stretched from Siberia to North America and acted as a bridge, allowing people to cross from one land to the other for the first time.

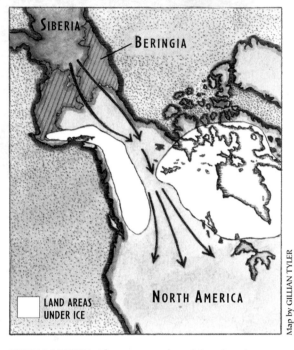

Map by GILLIAN TYLER

FIRST FOOTING: The route people took into America.

MOVING TO PASTURES NEW

People didn't suddenly flock across the bridge, of course — it was a gradual process. Siberian hunters moved to Beringia only when they found it was warmer than Siberia.

The land was flat and criss-crossed with rivers that were full of fish. Moose and bison grazed on the wiry grass, and the hunting was good.

And slowly, as they followed game animals, the hunters edged south across Beringia, until finally they reached the top of North America.

Until then, America had been totally empty of people, but now fate and the freezing weather had made it possible to enter this great new land. And, pushing their way down past the ice-sheets that still gripped its coastal edges, group after group made its way south.

Now in 8,000 BC, we are no longer living in an ice age. The sea levels have risen once more and the land bridge has disappeared. But Beringia served a purpose — for without it, America would still be an empty and unexplored land.

CLOSER

me that winter in their lands now lasts for nine months of the year, and that even in summer the hunting is barely good enough to keep them alive.

But this is not a new story. The same thing is happening in Germany, Belgium, Britain and northern France, too — and people are flocking south towards the coast of the Mediterranean.

And the reports from other parts of the globe are just as grim. Ice-sheets from the South Pole have spread nearly as far as Tasmania. Most of Australia is so cold, dry and windswept that people have been forced towards the coasts — the only place in Australia where it still rains.

Where will it all end, I wonder? I can't help thinking that if this terrible weather continues, the whole world will turn into a solid block of ice! 🐾

REWARDS FOR THE BRAVE: Just to the south of North America's icy mountains lies a hunter's paradise.

A LAND OF PLENTY

Illustrated by PETER VISSCHER

TODAY, IN 8,000 BC, America is once more cut off by a vast sea. But back in 11,000 BC, one of our reporters crossed the Beringia land bridge, to interview a young man about the American way of life.

"MY FATHER WAS born in Beringia — that's the land bridge from Siberia to America, you know. And when he was young, his group ventured further east than usual one year, following some caribou.

Eventually, they found they'd left Beringia far behind them and entered Alaska. But the winter there was too cold, so they headed on south.

For many weeks, vast walls of ice hemmed them in on either side. Then snowy mountains appeared up ahead, and they began to fear that their way was blocked. But they kept going and eventually their courage paid off. On the far side of the mountains lay a vast plain. Our group has stayed in this area ever since, and it's here that I was born.

WEIRD WILD ANIMALS

Now and then, people pass through here on their way south, but I've never felt tempted to go any further myself. There are so many big animals to hunt here — bison, camels and antelopes to name just a few. So there's more than enough food to keep my family group happy.

The old people in my group tell me that they'd never seen such animals before they came here. And because the animals had never seen humans either, they were so tame that the hunters could virtually walk right up to them and take their pick!

This isn't the case any longer, of course, but hunting is still pretty easy here. And if we ever want a bit of excitement, we can always go after some of the more dangerous creatures — like bears or tigers or even mammoths.

Believe me, America is a hunter's heaven, and there's plenty of space for more people to come over and join us. It's a real land of opportunity!"

NEW-FANGLED FARMING

Illustrated by SHARIF TARABAY

THIS SPECIAL REPORT, first printed in 8,400 BC, broke the hottest news story of recent times. In it, our Middle East reporter describes a new way of gathering food that's been developed there — called farming.

I'D HEARD A rumour that some people in Syria were experimenting with a new way of producing food, and that instead of following the herds like the rest of us, they were living in one place! I just had to investigate this strange behaviour.

When I arrived, one of the women offered to show me around. She took me to an area where hundreds of tall plants were growing in clusters. I recognized them as wheat, rye and barley, but I'd never seen so many growing this close together before. Usually, you find just one or two small clumps at a time. I asked my guide to tell me how these big clusters of plants had come about.

SEEDS OF SUCCESS

Apparently, some years ago, the climate in this region became extremely dry. Reliable sources of water were harder and harder to find, so people couldn't roam as widely as they once had. Instead,

REAPING THE BENEFITS: Harvesting a field of grain is hard but rewarding work.

they were forced to remain close to rivers.

Because they could no longer go far in search of food, they started to build up a store of grains to last them through the winter months. Then, one spring, they noticed how some grains that had been dropped on the ground had sprouted.

As an experiment, they tried spilling more seeds, this time on land they had cleared by gathering wild grain the previous year. It took several attempts, but at last they managed to grow their own plants. Now they scatter grain each spring.

When the seed-heads become ripe, they are cut off using curved, flint-bladed knives. The grain is then separated from the husks and spread out to dry in the sun, before being stored in baskets.

I was astounded by all that I had seen. The more I thought about it, the more this farming idea made sense. It could change everything! Just think, we could settle in one place and grow our own food plants, as the people here do. Then we wouldn't have to spend all those long autumn days scouring the land for enough wild food to last through the winter. And whenever animals are scarce and the hunting poor, there will still be a supply of food at home.

Stone Age people are often set in their ways, but you have to move with the times. And I, for one, hope that this newfangled farming catches on! ✉

DO YOU THINK IT'LL GROW?

Cartoon by JAMIE CHARTERIS

THE MOMENT OF VICTORY: Hunters succeed in chasing a herd of bison into a dead-end gully.

BISON BONANZA!

Illustrated by GINO D'ACHILLE

THE TASK OF catching enough food to feed the family through the winter is a problem we've all faced. But now, mass-kill hunting offers a solution. Read our reporter's inside story of an autumn bison chase.

THE SUN HAD only just risen when I joined the rest of the hunters for the big event.

I was struck by the huge number of people gathered here on North America's Great Plains — close to 100, including women and young boys. It was a far cry from the small groups in which we usually hunt.

Our hunt leader had told me that a herd of bison was known to pass this way every autumn.

The plan was to trap the herd in a narrow, steep-sided gully. It was a dead-end, so there'd be no escape for them.

We were gathering our weapons when a look-out ran up to say that the herd had been spotted.

The leader sent a handful of hunters to wait on the far side of the gully. The rest of us were told to form a loose semi-circle behind the herd. Then, on a sudden signal from the leader, we sprang into action, waving our spears and shouting.

The startled bison stampeded away from us, straight into the gully. And, finding themselves trapped, they panicked, trampling the smallest and weakest animals underfoot. Some tried to escape up the sides of the gully, but the hunters on the bank pushed them back in with their spears.

IN FOR THE KILL

Our group sent a shower of spears flying down on the animals. Many of the bison lay dying as we ran in closer to the remaining beasts and stabbed them. And, by the end of the afternoon, every bison in the herd had been killed.

As I gazed at the mountain of meat before me, I was struck by the ease and speed with which the mass-kill had happened. Once cut up and dried, there would be enough food here to keep our family groups well-fed for months.

Hunting together like this, instead of in small bands, was clearly the key. Tired, but proud of our victory, we still faced the task of dividing up our meat and hauling it home. But first, there was something far more important for us all to organize — a huge feast of fresh roast bison! ◪

HUNTING HOTSHOTS

Illustrated by MAXINE HAMIL

OUR HUNTING HELPLINE has been giving our readers great advice for a very long time. Here, we reprint our responses to some of your most frequently asked questions.

? I don't have any luck catching birds. What's going wrong?

TANGLED: Birds caught out.

Scatter some grain and wait until the birds are eating. Then hurl a fine net over them. It should be weighted with stones so the birds can't lift it and escape.

? Which is the best weapon to use to hit a distant target?
It's that old debate — traditional spears versus new bows and arrows. Many hunters think that spears are easier to aim, but others claim arrows are quicker to use and better in woodland. We say both are equally good for killing, so it's up to you.

? What's the best way to trap small, speedy animals, such as hares?
It's very simple. Make a looped snare by tying a slip-knot in a piece of plant-fibre rope.

Hang the rope from a tree along a route that you know hares often use. Weight the snare down with a twig and leave some bait beside it.

When the animal jumps on the twig, the knot will tighten round its leg. The hare will be unable to escape. **?**

LOOK OUT!: An unsuspecting hare approaches a snare.

A DOG'S LIFE

TODAY IN 8,000 BC, many of us keep hunting dogs. But how many readers know that our friendly pets are related to that ferocious animal, the wolf? This article from 2,500 years ago tells how it all began.

IT'S AMAZING, but it's true — humans and wolves, two completely different species, are living side by side!

Hunters in northern Europe have now reared litters of wolves that enjoy human company and even obey their owners' commands.

PUPPY LOVE

The idea of taming wolves happened by chance, when children found some abandoned wolf cubs while out playing. They took the cubs home, fed them scraps, and cuddled and fussed over them.

We're so used to being terrified of wolves that we can't think of them as pets. And yet contact with humans tamed these wild cubs.

Instead of running away as soon as they were old enough to hunt for themselves, these wolves seemed to look upon the children as their "family". They joined in the children's games, and even tried to copy some human expressions by curling their lips into a smile. Now, no wild wolves would do that!

When the children grew older and joined in the hunting, their pet wolves went along too.

Naturally, the wolves had very good hunting instincts. Not only did they enjoy the chase, but they could sniff out animals hiding in trees or bushes and then hold them prisoners there for their owners to kill.

Once other hunters had seen how useful these tame wolves were, they got wolf cubs of their own. People and dogs — could this be the beginning of a beautiful friendship? **?**

BEST OF FRIENDS: Children play with their pet wolf cub.

MAKE THE MOST OF A MAMMOTH

Illustrated by BEE WILLEY

MAMMOTHS ARE EASY enough to spot, but as everyone knows, they're very difficult to catch. That's all the more reason to make the best use of a freshly killed mammoth when you've got one. *The Stone Age News* offers some handy hints on how to make the most of your mammoth!

1 MEAT

○ Offer what you can't use to others and impress them with your generosity.

3 BONES

○ Use the biggest ones to build a strong frame for a hut.

5 FAT

○ Eat it – it's great for giving you extra energy.

○ In cold weather, rub some fat on your skin to keep the chill out.

○ Make a lamp by putting some fat in the hollow of a stone. Use a piece of twig as a wick. Set light to the wick to create a lovely, warm yellow glow.

6 BRAINS

○ Raw brains are a welcome treat for old people and children, because they're so easy to chew.

○ Rub them into hides. This will soften the leather, making it easier to sew into clothes.

7 TUSKS

○ The ivory bone of the tusks is very valuable, so keep some back to trade.

○ Carve it into little statues or amulets.

○ Shape it into beads.

○ Sharpen it with a knife to make hard, deadly spearheads.

8 TONGUE

○ The flesh of a mammoth's tongue is very tasty. Remove the rough, bristly skin from the tongue and slice the flesh into small pieces. Give it to toothless old people and toddlers. They can suck the goodness from it and spit out any bits that they can't chew.

- Eat it raw or roasted – it's delicious!
- Cut some raw meat into strips and dry them in the sun. They will keep for months.
- Treat your dogs to a few scraps.

2 BLOOD

- Drink as much as you can while it's still fresh.
- Add it to stews to thicken the sauce.

4 HIDE

- Rub the furry side with fat to make it waterproof and use it as a tent covering.
- Wear it. Mammoth hide is thick and heavy and makes a good cloak for cold weather.

- Use smaller bones to support skewered meat as it cooks over a fire.
- Bits of bone can be carved into sharp needles, or spearheads.

9 SINEWS

- Use the stringy bits of muscle – the sinews – as thread to sew pieces of hide together for tent coverings.
- Use them to bind flint- or bone-blades on to wooden handles to make weapons such as spears.

10 FUR

- Plait or twist longer strands to make rope or string.
- Tie tufts of it to your clothes – a fur trimming not only looks good, but helps keep out the cold.

A GOOD CATCH

Try our deadly harpoon blades. Just strap one to a stick and stab. No fish will be able to escape the new, specially carved, jagged barbs.

GET HOOKED, SOUTH-WEST FRANCE

TRACKERS' WORKSHOP

LEARN HOW TO:

- IDENTIFY ANIMALS BY THEIR PAWPRINTS.
- TELL FROM LOOKING AT LEAVES AND GRASS HOW LONG AGO A HERD PASSED BY.
- MAKE THE LATEST TYPES OF TRAPS.

VISIT US WHEN PASSING THROUGH BRITAIN'S THAMES VALLEY.

Charming!

Lost confidence in your skills at the chase? Do you want to improve your hunting and impress the rest of your group? Charm your way to the top with our mammoth-bone amulets! Guaranteed to bring you luck!

◇ LITTLE CHARMERS, SIBERIA, NORTHERN ASIA ◇

BURNING ISSUES

Illustrated by CHRIS MOLAN

COOKS THESE DAYS have more ways of preparing food than ever before. But can you really beat a good old-fashioned roast? *The Stone Age News* asked a traditional cook and one who prefers to experiment with new recipes to explain their views.

THE FAMILY ROAST: A tradition to be proud of.

THE TRADITIONALIST

"I'm a firm believer that the old ways are the best. Roasting is a tried and trusted method. Why waste any precious food trying out new ways of cooking that might not even work?

You can roast a piece of meat anywhere. All you need do is skewer it on a wooden spit and find a couple of supports to raise it above a fire.

It's a sociable way of cooking, too. My family group likes nothing better than to gather round the fire for a chat while they wait for the hot, juicy strips of roast meat to be sliced off the joint.

And while the meat is roasting, you can watch to make sure it cooks to perfection. With this new style of cooking, I've heard you put all the food in a bag. It must be nerve-racking not being able to tell if the food inside is raw or cooked."

THE EXPERIMENTER

"It's true that traditional roasting produces good results, but I get bored with cooking the same dish every day. I like to try out new ideas. My favourite at the moment is the 'boil-in-the-bag' approach. It's really easy.

First you need to make a cooking pit by digging a hole in the ground. Then lay a thick piece of hide over the hole and push it down so that it forms a waterproof liner.

Next, carefully clean out an animal stomach, pack it with food, and tie it up very tightly so that nothing can leak out.

Fill up the hole with water and bring it to the boil by dropping in red-hot stones that have been heated in a fire. When the water is boiling, you simply add the parcel of food and let it cook.

The meat boils in its own juices and makes a lovely, rich stew. And you can vary the taste by putting herbs and spices, or even vegetables and fruit, in the parcel, too. Try reindeer and beans, or water bird with berries and garlic!

My family group really looks forward to meal-times now — everyone loves trying to guess what's in each new dish.

You know what they say, 'Variety is the spice of life'. Well, that's always true with a boil-in-the-bag stew!"

BOIL-IN-THE-BAG: A new way of cooking that's really stirring things up!

GOT A SWEET TOOTH?

IF SO, WE HAVE THE ANSWER!
By cutting into the bark of our specially chosen trees, we can collect delicious sweet liquids. Try our favourite – maple syrup. Or you might prefer the sugary delights of birch, black walnut, hickory or butternut.

BEATS HONEY ANY DAY!
SUGARY SWEET, MAPLE GROVE, NORTH AMERICA

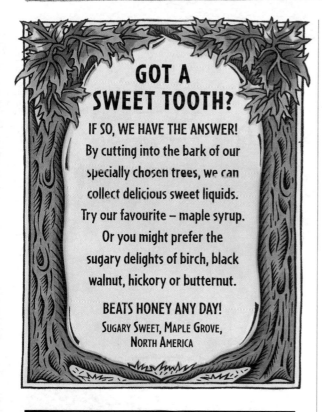

SPICE UP YOUR LIFE!

Are your meals as tasty as they could be? Choose from our huge range of spices and flavourings, including coriander seeds, juniper berries, basil and garlic.

SPICY EXTRAS, SOUTHERN INDIA, ASIA

PERFECT PEMMICAN

THE ANSWER TO EVERY TRAVELLER'S NEEDS — IT'S EASY TO CARRY AND KEEPS FOR DAYS. MADE FROM TOP-QUALITY SUN-DRIED MEAT AND BLUEBERRIES, CHOPPED AND MIXED WITH MOOSE FAT. ONE SMALL PIECE MAKES A MEAL.

MADE-TO-LAST FOODS, ROCKY MOUNTAINS, NORTH AMERICA

GRANNY'S KITCHEN

Illustrated by EMILY HARE & MIKE WHITE

THEY SAY THAT experience is the best teacher! So why not learn some handy hints from Granny, our food expert, who has been feeding a hungry family for many a year?

IT'S THE SAME every autumn — piles of food all ripening at once and not enough time to eat them. But there are ways to make food last longer. Try some of these.

● Drying is a good way to make sure you have a stock of fruit and vegetables for winter.

Cut them into small pieces and put them on flat stones or wooden platters in a clean, airy place. Make sure the pieces don't touch one another — they dry much more quickly if the air can flow all around them. If the weather's bad, leave them to dry near a fire.

● You can dry fish and meat, too. Cut the flesh into thin strips. Most people leave them to dry outside, but I prefer to hang them over a fire, as the strips dry more quickly and the smoke seems to give them a pleasant taste, too.

● When all your food has dried, store it on some grass mats or in baskets raised above the ground. Try to keep everything very dry.

● And do remember to put aside some grains, such as wheat, barley and maize, to see you through the winter. It's so important to have a properly balanced diet. Store them in baskets beside your stock of dried foods. Eat well this winter!

FLINTKNAPPER KNOW-HOW!

Illustrated by IAN THOMPSON

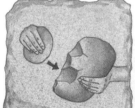

1 First, I use a stone hammer to chip out a basic shape called a core – I'll get lots of blades from this.

2 Next, I level off one end of the core. This gives me a striking platform to use when I get to step 4.

3 Then I use a soft antler hammer to chip a ridge all the way down one side of the core.

4 Starting at the level end, I work around the core, chipping off long "blades" of flint.

5 Taking one blade at a time, I tap around its edges to sharpen and shape them.

6 And this is what I'm aiming for – a perfectly pointed and deadly spear-blade!

FOR THIS EXCLUSIVE interview, *The Stone Age News* managed to track down one of the most respected flint-workers of our age. Here, he reveals his pride in his craft — and some of his trade secrets!

❓ Does it take long to learn to flintknap?

Oh, yes — mastering how to chip and shape flint is a lifetime's task! It's not surprising that only a few men in each family group choose to make it their particular craft.

I began when I was still a young lad. At first, I just watched the flint-knappers at work. Later, they taught me how to shape the flint into tools. And I'm still improving my technique, even today.

❓ So what makes a good flintknapper?

You've got to have a feel for flint and be able to judge a good piece. It mustn't be cracked by heat or frost, or it won't break cleanly.

I always tap a new flint with a pebble. If it gives a nice clear ring, I know it's a good one. If it makes a dull thud, I throw it away.

Flint's never easy to handle, so you also have to be extremely patient and able to concentrate hard on the job in hand.

It takes only a single bad strike to shatter a flint and send dozens of needle-sharp fragments flying through the air. People have been blinded in this way!

❓ What's so special about flint?

Quite simply, I think flint makes the best tools. It's harder and sharper than wood or bone. And if it's treated with care, a flint tool will last much longer.

I have heard that flint isn't found in some parts of the world and that other types of rock are used instead. But I don't know much about that.

To my mind, nothing beats flint. Okay, so I'm prejudiced! But I even like the way it looks and feels. Flint comes in lots of shades, from black to pale grey, and it's so wonderfully smooth and cool to the touch! It's simply the best! **R**

A CHALLENGE!

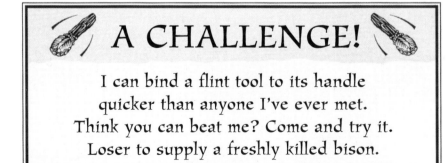

I can bind a flint tool to its handle quicker than anyone I've ever met. Think you can beat me? Come and try it. Loser to supply a freshly killed bison.

✋ Find me at Death Valley, North America ✋

CALLING ALL FLINTKNAPPERS

COME TO US FOR:

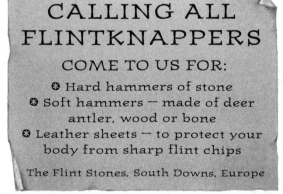

✪ Hard hammers of stone
✪ Soft hammers — made of deer antler, wood or bone
✪ Leather sheets — to protect your body from sharp flint chips

The Flint Stones, South Downs, Europe

ALLEYN'S SCHOOL LIBRARY

ALLEYN'S SCHOOL LIBRARY

THE IDEAL TOOL KIT

Illustrated by MAXINE HAMIL

KNIVES

Knives are our most important tools. There are many kinds, but some are more useful than others.

These are the best ones to have — small, thin knives for carving wood and bone, long knives for hunting, and short, sturdy knives for chopping up meat.

A CUT ABOVE: Use a small knife to shape wood.

SCRAPERS

Most of us use these rounded blades simply for scraping the flesh from animal hides. But they are handy for other tasks as well, such as smoothing the surface of a bone or antler tool, for example, or making a hollow in a block of wood to use as a bowl.

WE'VE COME A long way since the time when handaxes were the only tools around. Nowadays, we have so many kinds of tool, we're spoilt for choice. So here, to make things simple, *The Stone Age News* presents a blow-by-blow guide to the top five tools.

MATCHING TOOL TO TASK: It's best to clean up an animal hide with a scraper.

Scrapers work best when they're bound to a wooden haft, or handle. This gives you a much firmer grip so you can work more efficiently.

BURINS

These narrow little blades are used for fine work. A burin is the only tool that will give good results when you want to shape small, delicate objects, such as

ART WORK: Burins are ideal for carving pictures.

needles or beads for necklaces. The single sharp point at the top

is perfect for carving delicate bone, antler and even ivory pieces. And when you have finished carving, apply the finishing touches by using a burin to engrave patterns or a picture on the piece.

And finally, because a burin also has a hard, sharp edge along one side, it can be used as a small scraper for removing bumps from pieces of bone.

AWLS

These long and pointed piercing tools are not used frequently, and yet they are essential.

Awls are best used for punching holes in hides before you sew them together. They're also good for drilling holes in bone beads.

TOP TIP: Awls are sharp — punch holes with care.

POINTS

How would our hunters manage without these strong blades on their spears? They are perfect for bringing down fierce animal prey.

Spear points can be made in various sizes and shapes. The most effective ones to use have sharpened edges on either side of the blade, rather than just on one side.

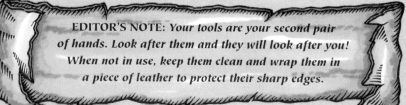

EDITOR'S NOTE: *Your tools are your second pair of hands. Look after them and they will look after you! When not in use, keep them clean and wrap them in a piece of leather to protect their sharp edges.*

FASHION

Illustrated by SUE SHIELDS

WONDERING HOW to keep your clothes up to date? If so, here's some timeless advice from the fashion editor of *The Stone Age News*. Apparently, there's more to real style than changing your image every season...

FUN FEATHERS: Jazz up a plain outfit with a few trimmings.

WHEN CHOOSING what to wear, most of us go for what's fashionable. After all, no one likes to be behind the times. Yet there are other factors to looking good that we sometimes forget, with disastrous results.

This may sound dull, but be practical about your choice of clothes, and insist on quality. You'll look better and feel more comfortable.

Follow my three "T" tips — Tunics, Trousers and Trimmings — and you won't go far wrong.

Trousers are easy to wear and practical for both men and women. And the basic square-cut tunic, either belted or worn loose, can easily be adapted to fit anyone, from a lean, wiry hunter to a pregnant woman.

But there's a world of difference between a pair of trousers or a tunic that has been beautifully cut and neatly stitched and some rough-and-ready

outfit held together by a few untidy and loosely laced leather thongs!

There is no excuse for cutting good hide badly. Stone knives are easy to obtain, so if yours are getting blunt, either sharpen them or simply replace them.

SHAPE UP!

If you're not sure how much hide you need, then either use an old worn-out tunic and pair of trousers as a basic pattern, or else borrow a fashionable version from a well-dressed friend and then copy it.

Choose just the right weight of hide, too. It's no good wearing a lovely but lightweight piece of soft chamois leather just

THE FINISHING TOUCHES

EVERYONE GETS a bit fed up with wearing old clothes. If you're in one of those moods, here's how to jazz up your image without sewing a thing.

◇ Jewellery, colourful face-paint and a smart hairstyle will make all the difference to your appearance. If you want a change, wear bright

bead necklaces to liven up your clothes. And if your tunic's gone all baggy, try using an old belt that's been newly decorated with shells.

◇ Plant seeds, animal teeth, various seashells, and even fish-scales can make interesting necklaces. Drill a hole in

each of the pieces and then thread them on to strings. The strings must be strong, so use either twisted plant fibres or strips of tough hide.

◇ Most men are happy to let their hair and beards grow as nature intended, but women

AND FLAIR

Cartoon by JAMIE CHARTERIS

because it's fashionable and then shivering all through the winter. A heavy mammoth-skin cloak may not be very glamorous, but it'll look better if it's well-cut and at least you won't freeze!

However, good sewing usually means acquiring good tools. For example, fine antler needles are hard to come by, but they are essential for sewing tidy seams.

Never risk damaging your needles — use a stone awl to make holes in the hide first and only use the delicate needle for pulling the thread through the holes.

Last, but not least, "the Trimmings". When decorating your clothes, make sure you don't get carried away on a wild flight of fancy. Again, you must always be practical.

Exotic seashells sewn around a neckline are pretty for a while, but they break easily, and once broken they'll make your outfit look a mess.

Feathers sewn on to an outfit look extremely attractive, but it's best not to overdo it. Alternatively, you could sew on little tufts of fur instead. They look just as good and, more importantly, they'll last for longer.

Your clothes speak volumes about the kind of person you are. So don't let yourself down. Remember that the key to looking great and feeling good is both quality and comfort. So remember, be chic, never shabby! ▰

DRESSED TO KILL: Sturdy clothing is practical for hunting.

prefer to create new styles. Nowadays, the fashion is for shoulder-length hair with a fringe. Many women with this style braid their hair to keep it off their faces when they are working and cooking.

◇ Face-paint is always colourful and dramatic for festivals and other special occasions. It's fun to experiment with a variety of colours. For example, finely crushed red or yellow ochres mixed with water make lovely bright paints. ▰

FABULOUS FOOTWEAR

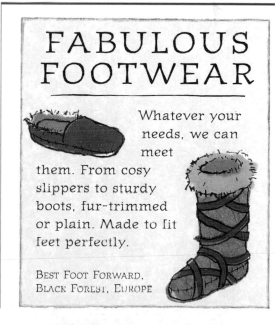

Whatever your needs, we can meet them. From cosy slippers to sturdy boots, fur-trimmed or plain. Made to fit feet perfectly.

BEST FOOT FORWARD, BLACK FOREST, EUROPE

A CAVE OF MY OWN

Illustrated by CHRIS MOLAN

SOME PEOPLE SEEM to have a knack for making a cosy home out of even the humblest hovel! *The Stone Age News* sent a reporter along to the South of France, to find out how one woman copes with cave living.

"OUR FAMILY GROUP discovered this cave in late summer and we've spent the entire winter here. The cave's size and location are just perfect.

It has plenty of room for all of us. There's a stream right outside, as you can see, and those trees on the hillside not only supply us with wood for burning and for making tools, but also shelter the cave from the worst of the wind and snow. Best of all, there's plenty of food — animals to hunt, and masses of nuts and berries to pick.

Now, do let me show you around. Mind your head, the entrance is low, but that makes it easier to defend, especially against fierce animals.

We always keep a fire burning in the entrance, too. I like to have a hot fire handy for heating up food. And I find that if you throw on a handful or two of pine needles and fan the smoke into the cave, it freshens the air and also helps to drive out sickness.

Here, you'd better take one of these lamps. It gets quite dark as you go deeper into the cave. I make the lamps myself — they're very simple, just a hollow stone, filled with burning fat, and a small thread of moss to act as a wick.

Like most caves, this one is a mixture of large chambers and passages. It stretches back for a very long way and has a lot more space than we need to use.

There are a number of passages leading off this main chamber, which in turn lead to more rooms.

HOME COMFORTS

Over here I've built a sleeping shelter — well out of the way of any draughts. It's basically just a wooden frame,

HOME SWEET HOME: Caves provide ideal shelter.

which I've covered with dried grass and propped against the wall. You can use turf or dried moss instead, but grass is the best for keeping the warmth in.

Inside the shelter, I've put thick hides on the floor — well-greased to keep out damp — as well as a few lighter furs for sleeping under. Most of us don't need shelters, but old people feel the cold more and like the extra warmth and comfort they give.

I've also organized some storage space. I use all the ledges for fragile items, such as baskets of dried berries and various herbs.

I've been so happy here this winter. But, of course, now that spring is coming we'll all be moving on soon, just as we always do. I'll miss this place, though. It's not always easy turning a cave into a home, but this one has certainly made my task much simpler. We'll definitely be coming back here next winter!" ◩

PERFECT PITCH

SADLY, ONLY THOSE of us who travel through hilly or mountainous lands can live in caves. But don't forget that tents can be almost as cosy — especially if you follow *The Stone Age News'* tips for placing and pitching them.

☻ Choose a sheltered, well-drained site, with a good source of water that's within easy reach.

☻ For a tepee-shaped tent, arrange wooden stakes in a circle and tie them together at the top. This construction is very stable, and if your poles are properly tied, there will be little chance of your tent collapsing on your head.

☻ Wind is your greatest enemy — a strong gust can easily leave you homeless! It's a good idea to place your tents side by side in a semicircle — to make an effective windbreak.

☻ Keep out wind *and* rain by using thick skins, such as bison hides, to cover the tent poles. The weight of the skins will also steady your tent during a gale.

☻ To stop skins flapping in the wind, put large stones around the bottom.

☻ Waterproof the skins by rubbing them with animal fat, and coat the seams with pine resin.

☻ As a quick alternative to a tent, make a lean-to by propping branches against a cliff face or boulder and cover it with hides. ◩

THE GOLDEN

Illustrated by SHARIF TARABAY

OLD MASTER: Our ancestors decorated their cave walls with living, breathing works of art.

ARTISTS CAN'T DRAW any more! That's what *The Stone Age News'* arts editor claims. Here, she compares the skills of today's painters with those of our long-dead ancestors.

THE ARTISTS of between 1,000 and 10,000 years ago knew how to paint well. The Golden Age of Art — that's what I call it.

These artists' vast and highly colourful portraits of animals just leap off the cave walls at you. Their bold use of line and paint makes their work so real you can almost see the beasts breathing!

EVERY PICTURE TELLS A STORY

When you look at the art of the past, you recognize what the artist meant to paint — you can tell whether it's a galloping horse, a jumping deer, or a charging bison.

But can you say the same about the art of today? Here we are in the year 8,000 BC, and all our artists want to do is decorate pebbles and other small objects with boring lines, squiggles, circles, dots and squares.

And what do all these geometric shapes and patterns mean? Can you tell me whether a squiggle is supposed to represent a river or a row of hills?

I'm afraid that your guess will probably be as good as mine. The truth

MODERN MADNESS: Does today's art have any meaning?

AGE OF ART!

is that no one, other than the individual artist, has a clue about what each piece of work is about!

And although so much time has passed that we can't really be certain, it seems as though the art of the Golden Age did have meaning.

There are people who believe that the painted caves were sacred places, and that when the artists of the past created their artwork, their intention wasn't just to copy what the animals looked like. It is thought that they were also trying to make contact with the animals' spirits, in the belief that this would help their people find animals to hunt for food.

LOST TALENTS

But it isn't just that the artwork of today lacks spiritual depth. It's my opinion that artists no longer know how to match the technical skills of our ancestors.

Their tools are made in much the same way, of course — tufts of moss and animal fur are still gathered, tied in clumps and attached to a piece of wood to make brushes. But today's methods of mixing up paints are definitely far less skilled than our ancestors'.

Black and red are the trendy colours today, but I believe this is simply because our artists have forgotten how to make any others! Where have all of the warm earthy yellows, deep reds, and browns of those stunning cave paintings gone?

Our ancestors knew just which rocks to grind into coloured pigments. And, through varying the amount of animal fat and water that they mixed with them, they achieved a range of richly glowing colours. The more animal fat they used, the glossier the paint became.

When I compare the art of today with that of the past, there's no doubt in my mind about which I'd prefer on my cave wall.

The magnificent cave paintings of the Golden Age of Art win hands down — every time! ▤

ONE TO TRY AT HOME!

1 Start by grinding a coloured pigment such as ochre into a fine powder. Heap it on a dish, and then mix it with animal blood or fat to bind it. Thin it by adding a little water.

COURTESY OF OUR arts editor, here's one of the techniques of those ancient artists that you can try on your own cave walls!

2 Use your hand as a mask to block out the paint. Place it flat against the wall with fingers spread out. Be careful not to move it!

3 Take a hollowed-out bone to use as a tube. Blow down it gently, to spray the paint evenly around the mask.

4 Lastly, remove the mask and admire your artwork! Now you have learnt the basic technique, you can try making other shapes by varying the number of fingers you show. ▤

FAMILY MATTERS

Illustrated by SUE SHIELDS

FAMILIES — YOU EITHER love them or hate them! And judging from reports that *The Stone Age News* has received over the years, sometimes you do both at the same time! Here, we reprint some classic family problems and solutions.

Q We used to be a typical, happy family group who all got on well together. That was before my brother's new woman came to live with us.

She's so selfish! When it's her turn to cook, she doesn't share the food out fairly. She saves the best bits for herself. What are we going to do about her?

A You've got a big problem! Sharing and caring are the basis of happy family life. Without teamwork, a family group can't hunt and work well together in order to survive.

You need to find out what is making this woman behave in such an antisocial manner. Has anyone been rude to her? Is she eating so much

MEAN TIME: One greedy person in a family is one too many.

because she's worried that we'll have yet another drought or cold spell, and there won't be enough food?

Everyone needs to eat, from the fittest hunter or cook to the oldest members of the group. No one has a right to more food than anyone else. It's vital that you find out why she's behaving like this and persuade her to stop.

Q I'm worried about my teenage son — he's so boastful! True, he's good at hunting, but he tells everyone just how great he is. We're getting fed up. I don't want to nag all the time, but his bragging must stop! What can I do?

A Your son will stop doing all this when he's older. Right now, it's a way of trying to fit in with others. Talk to him tactfully, as he must learn not to annoy other people.

We always hunt in small groups and never alone, so teamwork is much more important for survival than individual skills. But don't squash his energy. That can be a positive quality!

BIG HEAD: Don't boast about your catch — roast it!

Q Recently, my baby girl has started to cry a lot. It can get very loud and I'm worried that she'll howl through our autumn hunting celebrations. How can I calm her down?

A Stop worrying, there's a very simple solution. Your baby is teething. New teeth are growing and hurting her. To ease the pain, take some of the sticky sap, or

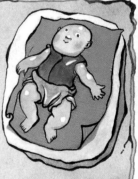

PEACE AND QUIET: No one likes a bawling baby.

resin, from a pine tree. Leave it to dry out a bit, then give a piece to her to chew on. I guarantee she'll quieten down.

Q Some of my group have reached the age of 45 or older! Several had important roles when they were a lot younger — two of them were hunt leaders, for example.

They looked after us and now it is our duty to care for them. The trouble is, they suffer from aches and pains and need a lot of looking after. What can we do to make them feel better and also lessen the burden on us?

WEAR AND TEAR: A lifetime's toil can take its toll.

A Sadly, old age brings a lot of pain and stiffness. You can't take the aches away, but you can soothe them by preparing a potion from stewed tarragon leaves and rubbing it into painful joints.

Otherwise, keep old people warm and well fed and, if they are too weak to walk, put a supportive arm round them or carry them on your back as you move camp.

Living with old people needn't be all give and no take. With all those years of experience behind them, aged family members are often a source of useful knowledge. Take an interest in them and above all, listen to what they have to say — you might learn something new!

IT'S YOUR FUNERAL

Illustrated by MAXINE HAMIL

DEATH COMES TO us all one day — so don't wait to the last minute to plan your funeral! Let *The Stone Age News* help you prepare, by guiding you through the range of burials currently available.

THE FIRST THING you need to decide is where you want your body to be buried.

Once, the only truly respectful place for a grave was inside a cave. But in the last 30,000 years or so, open-air sites have become a common alternative.

That's the easy part, though. There's a whole range of options about what happens next.

Your grave could be lined with a piece of animal hide and your body laid on top. Or you could be wrapped in the hide, and then put in the grave. And you could be placed on your front, back or side.

You might also like to have powdered red ochre dusted over your body to decorate it.

Last, but not least, decide whether any of your belongings (such as favourite items of jewellery or treasured tools) are to be buried with you. Who knows? They may be useful in the next world!

THE LAST WORD

And for those of you who want something really different, a new funeral practice has developed in Australia. They call it cremation, and it involves burning the dead body and then burying the ashes.

The choice is yours, of course, but just make sure you don't leave the decision too late!

FINISHING TOUCHES: A sprinkling of red ochre adds style to any burial.

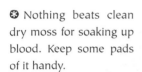

BE PREPARED!

DISASTERS WILL HAPPEN — mischievous toddlers will fall over, greedy youngsters will eat too much, and reckless hunters will have accidents. Here are some ideas for cures, as well as tips for keeping a well-stocked medicine kit. Make sure you're ready for the worst!

✺ Nothing beats clean dry moss for soaking up blood. Keep some pads of it handy.

✺ Make sure you have salt, crushed ochre and honey in stock — spread any one of them on a wound, to stop infection.

✺ Animal fat will soothe burned or chapped skin.

✺ Make a skin cream by mixing animal fat with red ochre. Use it to keep away flies and insects that sting.

✺ Stop indigestion before it even starts! Add a little chopped ginger root to your cooking — it won't just help to prevent tummy ache, it will also make your meals tastier.

✺ You'll be familiar with cumin and coriander only if you live in sunny lands. Those of you who do live in a warm climate should keep a selection of seeds from these two plants close to hand. When indigestion sets in, you can ease the pain by chewing these seeds.

✺ Look after your teeth by chewing on sap from pine trees to loosen any bits of food that get stuck.

✺ What could be worse than a bad headache? Stew up some dried rue leaves in water, for a drink to soothe the pain.

✺ For another calming, pain-relieving drink, boil some small pieces of willow-tree bark in water and sweeten with honey.

✺ Stewing dried catmint leaves in water won't just give you a delicious hot drink — you'll also be making an excellent cure for colds.

✺ If you catch a cold, you'll probably also get a sore throat. To ease the pain, make a mouthwash by boiling the inner bark of a plum tree in water.

✺ Soak dried camomile flowers in hot water, then let the liquid cool. Strain it, then rub it into your gums to help soothe the pain of a toothache.

✺ Illness can spread like wildfire. Burning dried sage leaves near the sick person may help — the smoke will prevent some diseases from passing to the rest of the family.

WARNING
These remedies *must only* be prepared by an adult!

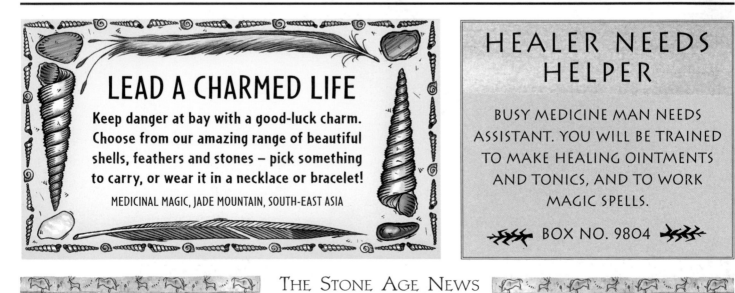

LEAD A CHARMED LIFE

Keep danger at bay with a good-luck charm. Choose from our amazing range of beautiful shells, feathers and stones – pick something to carry, or wear it in a necklace or bracelet!

MEDICINAL MAGIC, JADE MOUNTAIN, SOUTH-EAST ASIA

HEALER NEEDS HELPER

BUSY MEDICINE MAN NEEDS ASSISTANT. YOU WILL BE TRAINED TO MAKE HEALING OINTMENTS AND TONICS, AND TO WORK MAGIC SPELLS.

⤜⤜ BOX NO. 9804 ⤜⤜

SWAP TILL YOU DROP: At the trade centre, you can barter precious raw materials, like mammoth ivory and seashells, for hand-made goods.

IT'S A FAIR TRADE

Illustrated by LEE MONTGOMERY

WE STONE AGE people adore rare and exotic goods — but where's the best place to get them? In 10,500 BC, *The Stone Age News'* roving reporter visited Europe's biggest trade centre.

WELCOME TO the banks of the River Rhine in central Germany, and the site of the best trade centre in Europe!

I'm surrounded by foot-weary travellers from north, south, east and west. And each family group has brought raw materials with them to swap for the high-quality goods made here.

I've come across one group, for example, who carried arctic fox furs and top-grade flint stones all the way from Belgium.

It goes without saying that the further something has travelled, the rarer and more valuable it is. I've seen things from as far afield as the Atlantic Ocean and the coasts of the Black Sea. But the most precious things of all must have been some beautiful seashells from the Mediterranean coast of France.

Such rare items will have changed hands a great many times on the way here, of course — no one group could have brought them so far.

So what goods can you get here, and where are they made? Well, on each riverbank there are two or three huts where the various craft-workers come to live and work for several weeks or even months at a time. These sites are where the serious bartering takes place.

In the couple of weeks I've been here, I've seen some top-quality goods, including sturdy flint tools, fine spearheads, superb leather shoes and fur-trimmed tunics.

And the jewellery is lovely, too — necklaces and headbands made from painted seashells, and beads carved from an exquisite black stone known as jet.

Making up my mind was hard, but in the end I traded two sets of reindeer teeth for a mammoth-ivory spearhead.

ALL THE FUN OF THE FAIR

There's more to this place than bartering, though. I've listened to some first-rate storytelling and eaten marvellous food.

In fact, if you're ever here yourself, make sure you try the local delicacy — the way they cook horse tongue will leave you speechless! 🔲

MADE IN JAPAN

Illustrated by CHRISTIAN HOOK

ALL FIRED UP: These new Japanese pots are the best thing since stone knives.

WE PRIDE OURSELVES on being the first newspaper with the big stories, and here we reprint one of our greatest "scoops". This sensational article appeared back in 9,000 BC, when it broke the news of a brilliant Japanese invention — pottery!

JUST WHEN YOU think life can't get any more exciting, along comes a brand new way of using a familiar old material.

I'm talking about clay. You know the stuff — it's the soft sticky earth that gets stuck between your toes when it rains!

Clay is what bakes into a hard crust beneath your cooking fire. Some artists have made statues and beads out of it, but no one has ever thought up any other use for it.

Not until now, that is! We have just received news of an amazing invention — pottery, the art of making useful cooking vessels, called pots, out of clay.

The Jomon people of Japan have proved that it's possible to turn lumps of clay into containers that are heatproof, water-tight and strong!

BASKET BARGAINS

Run out of storage space again? On the move and need something light and easy to carry? Come and get one of our beautiful baskets made from willow or alder twigs. Various shapes available.

◇ Better Baskets, Black Forest, Northern Europe ◇

FEELING ROPEY?

Whether it's stringy plants, like hemp or flax, or the inner bark of trees — we've everything you need for plaiting or twisting the perfect rope.

FIND US AT THE DEAD SEA, MIDDLE EAST.

These fantastic Jomon pots are cone-shaped and usually a reddish-brown in colour. Often they're decorated with scratched patterns.

To cook with them, the Japanese simply fill them with food and water and place them in a fire.

And I'm told that the Jomon speciality — baked fish with herbs and a local vegetable called bamboo shoots — is delicious!

PERFECT POT: Not just pretty, but practical, too!

TRADE SECRETS

But I'm not just going to describe this wonderful invention. I can also reveal how the pots are made.

Jomon potters start by kneading a lump of clay until it softens. Then, with the palms of their hands, they shape small balls from the clay.

Some of these are moulded into a cup-shaped base. Others are rolled back and forth to form long, sausage-like shapes, which are wound around the base to build up the sides of the pot.

After smoothing the pot's surface by rubbing their fingers across the clay, the potters may decorate it by pressing a pattern into it with a stick or their fingers.

The pots are left for several days, until the clay is completely dry. Then comes the final,

most exciting stage — baking the pots in a big bonfire until they are rock hard.

The pots are carefully arranged on the hot ashes of an earlier fire. Then wood is piled over them and set alight.

Building the fire and keeping it going takes great skill, as any sudden change in temperature will crack the pots.

Finally, after around five hours, the piping-hot pots are pulled out of the glowing embers with a long stick, and placed in rows to cool.

So there you have it. There's only one question left unanswered — will this exciting new Japanese idea catch on and sweep the world? Who knows — only time will tell! 🔲

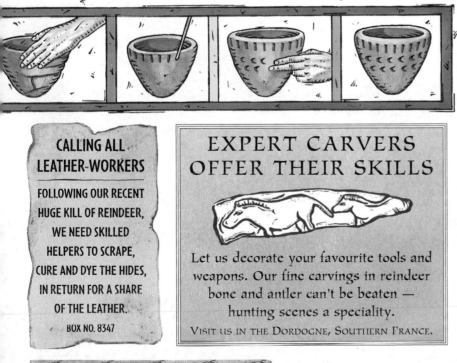

CALLING ALL LEATHER-WORKERS

FOLLOWING OUR RECENT HUGE KILL OF REINDEER, WE NEED SKILLED HELPERS TO SCRAPE, CURE AND DYE THE HIDES, IN RETURN FOR A SHARE OF THE LEATHER.

BOX NO. 8347

EXPERT CARVERS OFFER THEIR SKILLS

Let us decorate your favourite tools and weapons. Our fine carvings in reindeer bone and antler can't be beaten — hunting scenes a speciality.

VISIT US IN THE DORDOGNE, SOUTHERN FRANCE.

YOUR CHANCE TO WIN!

PRIZES TO BE WON IN OUR COMPETITION

WHAT CAN TOP A JOMON POT? THE STONE AGE NEWS CHALLENGES BUDDING DESIGNERS TO COME UP WITH A NEW STYLE OF CONTAINER. BIG OR SMALL, FOR LIQUIDS OR SOLIDS, AND IN ANY MATERIAL YOU CHOOSE — JUST MAKE SURE IT'S USEFUL!

FIRST PRIZE:
A GENUINE JOMON POT — OUR LUCKY WINNER WILL BE AMONG THE FIRST PEOPLE OUTSIDE JAPAN TO OWN THE LATEST DESIGN!

FOR RUNNERS-UP:
MANY OTHER VALUABLE PRIZES OF WEAPONS, JEWELLERY AND FOOD.

JUDGES WILL BE VISITING YOUR AREA FROM MIDSUMMER DAY, 8,000 BC, ONWARDS.

YOUR CHANCE TO WIN!

ADVERTISEMENT SPECIAL

WANT TO MAKE A SONG AND DANCE?

Every party needs music! Come to us for a fantastic range of instruments.

WHISTLES: made from bird, caribou or bear bone and giving a wide range of notes.

DRUMS: made from mammoth shoulder blades – for a loud, foot-tapping beat.

RATTLES: shake it up with our fabulous dried-out gourds – they're full of hundreds of seeds. Painted or plain ones available.

Whatever the occasion, shake, rattle and roll with our easy-to-play music-makers! They're simply the best.

drums · whistles · rattles

Contact the Melody Makers, Grand Canyon, North America.

STAND OUT FROM THE CROWD!

If you have a special ceremony ahead, come to us for your face- and body-paints. We have the best brown and yellow ochre colours you've ever seen. They're bright and very festive. Be bold, be beautiful!

COLOUR-ME GORGEOUS!
Black Forest, Europe

GIVE IT A WHIRL!

CALL ATTENTION TO YOUR CELEBRATION WITH ONE OF OUR NOISE-MAKERS. SIMPLY WHIRL THE DISC ON A STRING ROUND YOUR HEAD TO CREATE A LOUD HUMMING SOUND. THE NOISE WILL WHIP YOUR GUESTS INTO A FRENZY!

IN-A-SPIN SOUND SYSTEMS, GREAT DIVIDING RANGE, AUSTRALIA

LIGHTEN UP!

MAKE YOUR CELEBRATION GLOW. WE CAN SUPPLY STONE LAMPS IN ALL SIZES, PLUS THE ANIMAL FAT FOR FUEL. OR TRY OUR LONG-BURNING TAR TORCHES.

SEE THE LIGHT, BLACK SEA, ASIA

TELLING TALES!

Roving storyteller willing to speak at any celebration. I can repeat outstanding hunting accounts, tell exciting travellers' tales and prepare spiritual stories for religious ceremonies.

FIND ME AT THE GREAT SANDY DESERT. AUSTRALIA.

SMALL ADS

HUNTERS: TRY OUR DEER STALKERS!

DISGUISE YOURSELF IN OUR CLOAKS OF RED DEERSKIN. GET CLOSER TO YOUR PREY THAN YOU EVER DREAMED POSSIBLE.

SKIN DEEP,
LAND OF THE
MIDNIGHT SUN,
NORTH EUROPE

WARNING!

TO ALL READERS WHO TRAVEL TO THE WEST COAST OF NORTH AMERICA: Beware of the tar pits in this region. There are wide stretches of liquid tar that are very sticky in warm weather. Do not, we repeat not, try to reach any trapped animals, or you will become stuck yourself.

ALL ABOARD!

OUR BOATS ARE THE BEST. WE HAVE STURDY DUG-OUT CANOES, HOLLOWED FROM A COMPLETE LOG, FOR TRAVELS AROUND THE SHORE. OR TRY A RAFT, MADE FROM LOGS STRAPPED TOGETHER, FOR A TRIP ON THE RIVER.

SHIPSHAPE
SUPPLIERS,
SNAKE RIVER,
NORTH AMERICA

⊕ **from 200,000 BC**
Modern humans (*Homo sapiens sapiens*) appear in Africa.

⊕ **about 125,000 BC**
Modern humans begin to leave Africa and spread into the Middle East.

⊕ **about 50,000 BC**
Modern humans travel from Asia into Australia.

⊕ **about 40,000 BC**
Modern humans first reach Europe.

⊕ **31,000 - 9,000 BC**
In Europe, artists create colourful paintings and carvings inside caves. The greatest examples of these works date from 18,000 BC onwards.

⊕ **about 28,000 BC**
The last Neanderthals (*Homo neanderthalensis*) are believed to have died out in Europe.

⊕ **about 23,000 BC**
The earliest-known clay statuettes are made in central Europe.

⊕ **about 16,000 BC**
The last major ice age reaches its height. This period is known as the Last Glacial Maximum. It is a time of intense cold, when huge ice-sheets spread slowly outwards from both the North and South Poles, causing great hardship to all human and animal life.

⊕ **about 13,000 BC**
The first modern humans reach North America. They travel from Siberia to Alaska across a land bridge of exposed sea-bed, called Beringia.

⊕ **about 11,000 BC**
Modern humans have now spread throughout North and South America.

⊕ **about 10,500 BC**
Hunters in Europe tame wolf cubs. After many years, these wild wolves become pet dogs.

⊕ **10,000 - 8,000 BC**
Large mammals die out across the world. Among the lost species are the North American camel, the European mammoth, and the giant wallaby of Australia.

⊕ **about 9,000 BC**
In Japan, the Jomon people finally perfect the art of making and firing pottery — a technique that they have been experimenting with for more than 1,000 years.

⊕ **8,800 - 8,200 BC**
The minor ice age known as the Younger Dryas has a severe effect on the world's climate. Harsh droughts in the Middle East force people to stay close to reliable water supplies, such as rivers, instead of roaming freely.

⊕ **about 8,400 BC**
People in the Middle East clear fields, plant rye, wheat and barley and collect up the grains. This marks the start of true farming. Over the next thousand years, farming spreads to other parts of the world as people begin to settle in villages and grow crops. In time, most abandon the nomadic hunting and gathering lifestyle altogether.

ABOUT PLACE NAMES

We do not know what names Stone Age people gave to the lands in which they lived. The place names used in this book, such as the Middle East or North America, are the ones we use today.

Author: Fiona Macdonald
Consultant:
Alison Roberts
 Dept of Antiquities
 Ashmolean Museum
 Oxford
Editor: Anderley Moore
Designer: Louise Jackson

Advert illustrations by:
Maxine Hamil 13tr, 13mr, 15tl, 16bl, 30t
Emily Hare 19br
Louise Jackson 15ml, 29m
Michaela Stewart 15bl, 19br, 28br, 30bm, 31tl
Ian Thompson 26bl
Peter Visscher 31bl
Mike White 13br, 28bl, 30bl

Decorative borders and small illustrations by:
Maxine Hamil 1, 4-5b, 6l, 7br, 18-19b, 21r
Emily Hare 26t
Sue Shields 11br
Michaela Stewart 21r, 29r
Ian Thompson 22l, 23r, 23b, 28-29m
Peter Visscher 5r, 6r
Mike White 5t, 22, 29t
Bee Willey 8b

With thanks to:
Artist Partners
Illustration Ltd
Temple Rogers

First published 1998 by Walker Books Ltd 87 Vauxhall Walk London SE11 5HJ

This edition published 2001

2 4 6 8 10 9 7 5 3 1

Text © 1998 Fiona MacDonald

Illustrations © 1998 Walker Books Ltd

Printed in Hong Kong

All rights reserved.

British Library Cataloguing in Publication Data

A catalogue record for this book is available from the British Library.

ISBN 0-7445-7716-0

UNCOVERING THE PAST

The people who specialize in finding clues about the past are called archaeologists. Part of their job is digging up things that lie buried in caves and other places where people lived long ago.

Among other things, archaeologists have discovered skeletons of Stone Age people, as well as animal bones from their meals, the tools and weapons they made, the jewellery they wore, and even the beautiful cave paintings they created.

Every year archaeologists find out more information. With each new discovery, they add another piece to the jigsaw-puzzle picture we have of life in Stone Age times.

ALLEYN'S SCHOOL LIBRARY